Freaky
Flowers

Freaky Flowers

D. M. Souza

Franklin Watts
A Division of Scholastic Inc.
New York • Toronto • London • Auckland • Sydney
Mexico City • New Delhi • Hong Kong
Danbury, Connecticut

To Melissa Stewart for first planting the seed

Note to readers: Definitions for words in **bold** can be found in the Glossary at the back of this book.

Photographs ©: Dembinsky Photo Assoc.: 13 (Claudia Adams), 27 (Richard Shiell), 5 left, 30; Larry Ulrich Photography: 41 (James Randklev); Photo Researchers, NY: 14 (Biophoto Associates), 6, 24, 25 (Geoff Bryant), 8 (Nigel Caittlin/Holt Studios), 43 (Oswald Eckstein/Okapia), 9 (Dennis Flaherty), 11 (Michael P. Gadomski), 40 (Gilbert Grant), cover (Claude Nuridsany & Marie Perennou), 23 (Rod Planck), 36 (Kjell B. Sandved), 45 (Merlin D. Tuttle/Bat Conservation International), 10 (Jerome Wexler); Visuals Unlimited: 18 (Jon Bertsch), 19 (Bruce S. Cushing), 5 right, 16 (Jeff J. Daly), 47 (Daniel W. Gotshall), 38 (Bill Johnson), 22 (Joe McDonald), 44 (Mark Newman), 50, 51 (D. Newman), 48 (Fritz Pölking), 33 (Prance), 21, 31 (Kjell B. Sandved), 28 (David Sieren), 2 (Barry Slaven).

The photograph on the cover shows a wild sage flower being pollinated by a bee. The photograph opposite the title page shows the flower of a devil's tongue plant.

Library of Congress Cataloging-in-Publication Data

Souza, D. M. (Dorothy M.)
    Freaky flowers / D.M. Souza.
        p. cm — (Watts Library)
    Includes bibliographical references (p.).
    ISBN 0-531-11981-5 (lib. bdg.)   0-531-16221-4 (pbk.)
    1. Flowers—Juvenile literature. [1. Flowers.] I. Title. II. Series.
QK49 .S675 2002
582.13—dc21   2001017573

Contents

Flowering plants range in size from the eucalyptus tree, shown here in full bloom, to the tiny floating duckweed.

Chapter One

Plant Champs

When you hear the word *flower*, the image of a rose, daisy, sunflower, or other common bloom probably comes to your mind. Did you know that more than 230,000 **species** of flowering plants grow around the world? They range in size from the 330-foot (100-meter) eucalyptus tree to the 0.04-inch (1-millimeter) floating duckweed. Flowers grow on mountaintops, in forests and meadows, and on Arctic tundras. They live in deserts and even on other plants. About half the world's flowering plants are found only in rain forests. Many are more freaky-looking than you could imagine.

A cotton crop with flowers (foreground) and puffy cotton bolls (background)

Smallest Flowering Plant

Some species of the **genus** *Wolffia*, found in ponds in the western United States, are so small that 250 of them can fit on a postage stamp. In Thailand, people eat a species of *Wolffia* known as *khai-nam* ("water eggs").

Flowering plants play a major role in our lives. They serve as decorations for homes and gardens and as gifts for loved ones. They provide foods such as cereals, beans, nuts, **fruits**, and vegetables. Without flowers, we would have no herbs and spices, nor would we have beverages such as coffee, hot

8

chocolate, and cola. Paper, cotton, and linen fabrics, as well as the dyes that color them, would be unknown. We would also lack perfumes, certain medicines, and drugs. Our lives would be very different.

The Mighty Seed

Millions of years ago, no flowers bloomed on our planet. Only the greens and browns of mosses, horse-tails, and ferns dotted the land. Then plants with seeds slowly began appearing. Each seed contained a supply of food, a protective seed coat, and an **embryo**, the beginning of a new life.

The first seed plants were **gymnosperms**, whose name means "naked seeds." The seeds of these plants are located at the base of **cones**, special reproductive containers that are familiar in forests. Present-day trees such as pines, firs, cedars, spruces, and giant redwoods are all members of this group.

All gymnosperms generally form seeds in the same way. In the pine, for example, male and female cones

The first plants to reproduce through seeds were gymnosperms. Shown here is a Virginia pine tree, whose seeds form at the base of its cones.

grow on the same tree. During the reproductive season, the male cones release immense clouds of pollen grains (male sex cells). These cells are blown long distances, and some reach female cones on other trees. The male cells eventually work their way to the base of scales on the cones, where they join female cells. A seed forms, and when the scales of the cone dry and separate, winged seeds ride the breezes. Those that land where conditions are favorable grow into new pine trees.

The next group of seed plants to develop were the **angiosperms**, plants whose seeds are "enclosed" in the heart of a flower. When they first appeared about 145 million years ago, angiosperms had no petals or bright colors, and, like gymnosperms, they reproduced with the help of the wind. Over

A cutaway of a hyacinth seed pod with one seed inside

time, these plants began forming partnerships with insects, birds, and mammals. Angiosperms took on new shapes, colors, and scents, increased in numbers, and spread across the land. Today about 90 percent of plants are angiosperms.

A Look Inside

The wild geranium is a good example for examining the basic parts of a flower. In the center of the bloom is the **pistil**, the female reproductive organ. The pistil is made up of several parts: the **stigma**, a sticky crown that will later branch into five arms; the **style**, or stem, which holds the stigma upright; and the **ovary**, a swelling at the base of the stem that is filled with **ovules**, or "little seeds."

The parts of a wild geranium are easy to identify. Located at the center of the flower are the pistil and stamens, the female and male reproductive organs.

Circling the pistil are **stamens**, the male reproductive organs of the plant. The wild geranium has ten stamens; most other types of flowers have fewer than twenty. Pollen is stored in the **anther**, a small sac that is supported by a thin stalk called the **filament**. Surrounding the stamens are petals of various colors. Below the petals are **sepals**, the outermost protectors of young buds that will later surround the ovary.

Not every flower contains all the same parts as the wild geranium. The flowers of grasses and stinging nettles, for example, have no petals. Magnolias lack sepals. The blooms of willows contain only male or female parts, but not both. Regardless of their parts, however, all flowers have the same function: to form seeds.

Matchmakers

Flowers cannot walk from place to place. If their male and female parts are ever to meet, most flowers need matchmakers called **pollinators**. Insects, birds, bats, and other creatures provide this service, and flowers attract their attention in several ways. Some flowers have bright colors that pollinators are

Self-Pollination

Self-pollination occurs when pollen falls from male to female parts of the same flower. This is the least desirable method of pollination because it results in offspring that are exactly like their parents and less likely to survive if conditions change. **Cross-pollination**, in which pollen is carried from one plant to another, ensures a greater variation of offspring.

certain to spot, and some give off irresistible perfumes. Others, especially those growing in cold northern lands, generate enough heat to make their blooms warm hangouts for beetles, flies, and mosquitoes.

To help flowers reproduce, pollinators must carry pollen from bloom to bloom. To make this task worthwhile, many flowers offer delicious snacks, such as **nectar**. Some even make two kinds of pollen—one to be carried and the other to be eaten by the carrier. Bees, butterflies, and moths get almost all of their nourishment from pollen, nectar, or both.

Flowers rely on insects, birds, and other pollinators to carry their genes from one plant to another. Here, a swallowtail butterfly pollinates a cone flower.

A bee picks up pollen as it feeds on an apple blossom.

Imagine a bee landing on an apple-tree blossom. As it moves from flower to flower gathering food, some of the pollen from an anther sticks to the insect's legs and later brushes off onto a stigma. Soon after the transfer, the pollen sprouts a long tube that grows downward until it reaches the ovary and the ovules. There the male and female cells join and begin dividing to form a seed. A supply of fats, sugars, starches, and other nutrients, as well as a protective covering, surround the embryo.

In time, much of the apple blossom falls to the ground, but the closed ovary, still on the tree, swells and develops into a fruit. Hidden inside the fruit is a seed. Given the right conditions, the seed will eventually grow into a new apple tree.

Big Families

Over the centuries, angiosperms have continuously evolved and changed. They have adapted to new pollinators, habitats, or both, and a mind-boggling variety of flowering plants has multiplied around the world. To make sense out of this diversity, scientists have organized angiosperms into more than four hundred families based on the structures of their flowers and fruits.

The rose family, for example, includes more than rose plants with their fragrant blooms. It also encompasses plants that bear apples, pears, plums, peaches, strawberries, and raspberries, as well as seventy-four species of trees and shrubs. Most members of the rose family are characterized by flowers with five sepals, five petals with wavy edges, and ten or more stamens.

The legume or pea family is one of the largest angiosperm families. It includes not only trees (locust and sandalwood), vines (wisteria, beans), and ornamentals (sweet pea), but also crops such as lentils, peanuts, alfalfa, and clover. Legume species have butterfly-shaped flowers.

Some flowering plants exhibit outlandish colors, shapes, scents, and sizes that lure suitable pollinators. Others, after being transported to harsh environments, adapted in novel ways. In the following pages, we will take a close look at a few of these freaky flowers and their partners in pollination.

A rose's large petals and attractive scent invite honeybees to stay for a while.

Chapter Two

Made for Each Other

Honeybees are the main pollinators of flowers. Because these insects use both scent and sight when searching for meals, many blossoms send out sweet fragrances and display bright colors to attract them. Bee-pollinated flowers have large petals that serve as landing platforms. Some petals are marked with special lines or shapes that point the way to the flowers' hidden nectar.

Flowers also enlist the help of other pollinators. Snapdragons, for example, are too tightly closed for honeybees to push open, and their nectar glands are beyond the insects' reach. Bumblebees, which have bigger, stronger bodies and longer tongues, are able to pollinate these flowers. Honeysuckle lacks landing platforms for bees, but moths can easily hover like humming-birds while performing their service. The size, shape, and color of each bloom give clues to its special matchmaker.

Mimics

Members of the orchid family produce flowers with unusual methods of attracting pollinators. The bee orchid (*Ophrys apifera*) not only looks like a bee, but also emits a scent similar

Is this a bee or a flower? Bee orchids benefit from an uncanny resem-blance to their pollinators.

to that of female bees. When male bees emerge several weeks before females, they are lured by the scent and attempt to mate with the flower. In the process, they are dusted with pollen, which the bees deposit when they fly to another orchid.

Bucket orchids *(Coryanthes speciosa)* so disguise themselves with heady perfume that male green metallic bees literally fall for them. When the flower opens, two glands begin producing a liquid that drips into a small, bucket-shaped structure. A heavy fragrance rises from the wax that lies near the bucket's rim.

Excited by the scent of the orchid, male bees swarm around the plant and try to land near the buckets. As they push and

The bucket orchid's heady fragrance lures male bees looking to mate.

Flavorful Seed Pod

One tropical orchid produces a seed pod known as the vanilla bean, which is used as a flavoring in many foods and beverages.

shove to gain a position, one of the bees falls into a bucket. His wings become so weighed down by the liquid that he cannot fly out, and instead he must crawl through a narrow tunnel to escape. As the bee moves toward daylight, he passes beneath masses of sticky pollen on the flower's anther. A sac of pollen attaches like a backpack to the space between his wings, and he carries the sac to another orchid.

Some orchids bear a close resemblance to butterflies; others look just like moths. Yet others give off the smell of rotting flesh, which tantalizes flies. Each type of mimicry increases the chances that some of an orchid's millions of seeds will take root and grow.

Hidden Flowers

Have you ever noticed that the gooey inside of a fig bar is peppered with crunchy little seeds? This is because edible figs (*Ficus*) consist of masses of tiny flowers. More than seven hundred species of these trees grow around the world, particularly in the tropics. Each tree produces bulbous structures called **synconia**, which are filled with hundreds of inside-out flowers that develop into minute fruits.

In 1882, several Smyrna fig trees, which produce large yellow figs with amber pulp, were brought to California from Turkey. After several years, the Smyrnas failed to yield a crop, and no one knew why. An American botanist finally discovered that the trees' flowers contained only female parts and needed pollen found in wild figs, or caprifigs. The carrier of

20

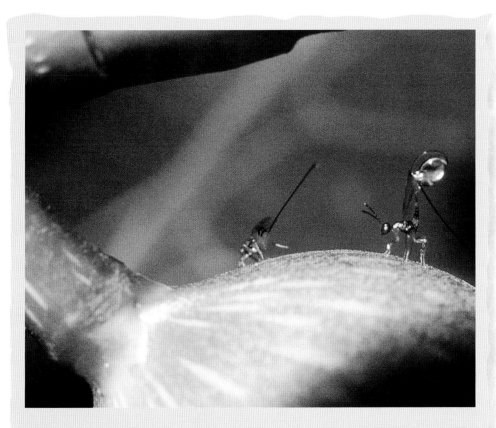

Fig Pollinator

The wild fig wasp is so small that it would fit through the eye of a sewing needle.

this pollen was a tiny wasp living in the wild caprifig. The wasp and its tree were quickly imported, and a few years later, the California trees began producing figs. Their fruit was given the name Calimyrna in honor of the Smyrna tree's new American home.

Each summer, the fig orchards of California are decorated with brown paper bags. Inside the bags are pollen-bearing wild figs and their special wasps. When the male caprifig flowers mature, the wasps, dusted with pollen, crawl out of their enclosures and begin laying their eggs inside the flowers of the Calimyrna trees. As they move from bloom to bloom, they pollinate each one. Seeds develop and soon turn into those crunchy structures that pose as fruit.

Long Bills and Tongues

Hummingbirds are perfectly suited to sip the nectar from trumpet-shaped flowers. Their bills are long enough to

A ruby-throated hummingbird pollinates hard-to-reach columbine flowers.

plunge deep inside the blooms of fuchsia, trumpet creeper, and similar flowers. Some of these flowers have special strategies that make certain the birds do their job while they are snacking.

Each spring, hummingbirds visit hundreds of jewelweed flowers *(Impatiens capensis)* that dot roadways and woodlands in eastern North America. The birds thrust their heads and long, pointed bills inside each blossom. The nectar lies a bit farther away at the base of a curved tube.

When the hummingbird sticks its bill inside the jewelweed and finds that it cannot reach its reward, it extends its tongue and curls it around the turn at the far end of the blossom. In doing so, it pushes its tongue against the flower. When the bird pulls its tongue in again, the flower swings back and drops pollen on the upper part of the bird's bill. Without this curve and push, the hummingbird might fly away without its supply of pollen.

Fruit of Jewelweeds

If you touch a jewelweed's pod-shaped fruit when mature, it shoots seeds in all directions. This is why the plants are commonly called "touch-me-nots."

The delicately shaped flowers of columbine *(Aquilegia canadensis)* face downward to prevent rain from diluting their nectar. Fortunately for the flowers, hummingbirds are able to

23

hover beneath the blooms and sip nectar with their long bills and tongues. As the hummingbirds feed, the flowers dust them with grains of pollen that are later carried to other columbines.

The blooms of organ-pipe cactus *(Stenocereus thurberi)* are a perfect match for bats. The white flowers open at night when the bats are out hunting for food, and their nectar flows freely enough to make it worthwhile for the bats to return again and again. Each time these mammals lap up the food with their long, bristly tongues, some of the pollen lands on their faces and necks. As they move to other flowers, it brushes off again. Mission accomplished!

Petal Posers

Many flowers have bright petals that attract pollinators, but some petals are so small that no creature can spot them. Have you ever noticed the flowers of poinsettias *(Euphorbia pulcherrima)*? The showiest parts of these plants are not flowers, but leaflike structures

A poinsettia's brilliant red bracts lure pollinators to the plant's tiny flowers.

known as **bracts**. Bracts attract pollinators that might otherwise not notice poinsettias' puny blooms.

Bracts act as road signs for dogwood blossoms and the flowers of fiery red Indian paintbrushes. They add to the total brightness of the tightly packed flower clusters of bee balm and clover. The three small flowers of the bougainvillea vine would scarcely be seen if it were not for three colorful bracts that pose as petals.

In Latin America, several species of wild banana plants produce bright yellow and orange-red bracts that hang like pendants on either side of a long stalk. After a time, the bracts bend upward to expose tiny flowers. Birds, drawn to the colors of the bracts, pollinate the blooms that eventually turn into a "hand," or cluster, of fruit.

Picky Plants

Some flowers welcome more than one kind of pollinator, but a few are more particular. Yuccas, which grow in the southern part of North America, have a unique relationship with a tiny moth. On summer evenings, the plants' waxy white flowers open. A female moth arrives, gathers sticky pollen from one flower, rolls it into a tiny ball, and carries it to another flower. There she drills a hole in the ovary wall and lays a batch of eggs. She flies out and presses the pollen ball into the cup-shaped stigma of the flower. When her young hatch, they eat a few of the developing seeds and leave the rest to grow into new yuccas. If anything happened to these moths, yuccas would soon disappear—and vice versa.

Witches

Early American colonists added the name *witch* to the hazel tree because they believed the late blooms were the work of witches.

Other flowers avoid competition when it comes to attracting pollinators. The witch hazel's spidery yellow flowers do not bloom until Halloween. By late October, the neighboring trees have dropped almost all their leaves and have no need for pollinators, so the witch hazel gets them all.

Jasmine attracts plenty of attention—both human and insect—with its heavy scent.

Chapter Three

What a Smell!

Lavender, honeysuckle, jasmine, and many other flowers are scented for the same reason that humans use perfume: to attract attention. While humans must purchase perfumes, flowers make their own. Scientists have discovered that some floral scents contain as many as sixty different chemicals.

Each flower's fragrance attracts specific pollinators. Musky odors bring bats, sweet-smelling ones lure bees, and heavy scents attract moths. Flowers that are pollinated by beetles, flies, and midges produce scents that are unbelievably stinky. Because these insects normally feed on dung, corpses, and decaying matter, flowers lure them with the smells of some of their favorite foods. These and other foul-smelling blooms reveal the lengths to which flowers go to attract pollinators. While the flowers are spectacular in size and shape, their smells keep them from ever becoming decorations for any home or office.

"Come into My Parlor"

Skunk cabbage (*Symplocarpus foetidus*) grows in swampy areas of the eastern United States and Canada. Its flowers, which bloom very early in the spring, are hidden beneath a purplish-

Skunk cabbage grows in the swamps of eastern North America. Like the poinsettia, this plant's flowers are upstaged by large bracts.

brown bract that acts like a leather overcoat protecting them from the cold. The plant gives off a foul odor that hints of the decaying flesh in which flies lay their eggs. The insects swarm over the plant, crawl inside its bract, and pick up grains of pollen as they deposit their eggs. When they fly to other skunk cabbages, the pollen rubs off, and the seeds of new plants begin to grow.

Hot Cabbages

Some skunk cabbages give off enough heat to melt the snow and ice around them.

Ancient Beliefs

During the Middle Ages, long before scientific names were given to flowers, the Dutchman's pipe caught the attention of herb gatherers in Europe. In the blossoms of the plant, they saw the likeness of an unborn child curled up in its mother's womb. They believed this was a sign that parts of the plant could be used in the delivery of babies. From this practice came the name *Aristolochia*, which means "best for delivery."

The tube-shaped flowers of the Dutchman's pipe (*Aristolochia gnaxima*) lure insects with their foul odor and then trap their pollinators to ensure reproductive success. The blooms of this plant grow upright and send out a putrid smell. Small gnats land and quickly slip on a waxy surface. They fall into the pipe, where thick, downward-pointing hairs prevent them from climbing out.

While imprisoned, the gnats are treated to nectar. Several days later, when the plant's pollen is ready, the hairs wilt, the flower tilts, and the pollen-covered gnats walk out of their jail. They fly away to another Dutchman's pipe, enter, and deposit the pollen.

The Titan

The record for the world's smelliest flower belongs to the titan (*Amorphophallus titanium*), a member of the Arum family. The titan is also one of the tallest and fastest-growing plants. Wherever it blooms, this relative of the skunk cabbage becomes a showstopper.

In 1878, an Italian botanist traveling in the tropical rain forests of Sumatra, Indonesia, discovered a flowering plant that was taller than any man. It had a huge, vase-shaped bract surrounding a towering central column known as a **spadix**. Thousands of flowers at the base of this column gave off a repulsive odor. Natives called it the "corpse flower" because it smelled like a dead body. Seeds of the plant were collected, and a few titans were later grown in Italy. Some of the plants

The titan plant, shown here at a height of over 6 feet (2 m), has the world's stinkiest flowers.

from Italy were shipped to the famous Royal Botanic Gardens at Kew, England, where a bloom created quite a sensation in 1889.

At first the interior of the titan at Kew was hidden, but within a few days, a ruffle-edged bract unwound, and a central column began growing above it. The bract then opened completely, exposing its maroon-violet inner surface and giving off a scent like that of rotten fish. Bottle flies swarmed over the plant, crawling inside to reach the flowers at the base of the bract. Viewers were stunned when the entire column began wilting after a few hours.

Several titans have since been grown in the United States. One bloomed in the New York Botanical Gardens in 1937 and drew crowds of curiosity seekers. It was over 8 feet (2 m) tall, and its bract was 4 feet (120 centimeters) across. So that they could examine the actual flowers, scientists cut a window near the base of the bract. More than four thousand ivory-colored male flowers were growing above several hundred yellowish-orange females. The spectacle lasted four days and then wilted.

In 1999, the eleventh recorded titan bloom in the United States drew about ten thousand admirers to the Huntington Botanical Gardens in San Marino, California. People waited in line for several hours just to see the strange plant. Fortunately, no one was overcome by its stench—although one boy wore a gas mask for protection.

Corpse Lily

Although the titan is huge, it is not the largest flower in the world. The award for size goes to the corpse lily *(Rafflesia arnoldi)*, named for the two men who discovered it in 1818. Its bloom is as large as a washtub.

Sir Stamford Raffles and Dr. Joseph Arnold, a naturalist, were on a botanical expedition in the jungles of Sumatra when they came upon something that looked as if it were from another world. A single flower 3 feet (1 m) in diameter was growing close to the ground under some bushes. It had no leaves or stems and was a fleshy red color splashed with creamy white spots. In the center of the flower was a bowl-like

Rafflesia arnoldi, *the corpse lily, is the largest flower in the world. It can weigh up to 25 pounds (11 kg) and measure 3 feet (1 m) in diameter.*

container large enough to hold several quarts of nectar. The bloom was anything but sweet smelling; flies hovered over it as they would over a dead animal. Arnold estimated that the flower weighed at least 15 pounds (7 kilograms).

Instead of making its own food as most green plants do, *Rafflesia arnoldi* lives as a **parasite** inside the stem of a vine. Occasionally a pale orange bud, resembling a cabbage, breaks through the vine stem and grows into a huge blossom that weighs as much as 25 pounds (11 kg). In place of petals are five fleshy sepals covered with white spots.

A single corpse lily produces as many as four million seeds, but the plant does not grow easily. Ants, squirrels, wild pigs, and even elephants carry the seeds from place to place, but seeds must land in a moist place on the host vine. Only if they break through the tissues of the vine will they grow and eventually produce massive flowers.

Familiar Parasite

Mistletoe is a parasite that grows on the branches of trees. It relies on its host for water and support.

The enclosed seeds of angiosperms allow the plants to reproduce far from where they grow. These trumpet flower seed pods are ready to be dispersed.

Chapter Four

Strange Habitats

Hooked seeds can cling to animal hide or hair and be carried miles away from where they first formed. Some seeds, like those of the coconut, ride ocean waves and end up continents away. Others are eaten by animals and dropped far away inside dung. Because of their enclosed seeds, angiosperms have been able to spread farther than any other type of plant.

Their tendency to travel has taken flowering plants to places with harsh

Ants attack other insects that try to feed on the bull's-horn acacia, pictured here. In turn, the plant's thorns serve as a shelter for the ants.

growing conditions. Slowly the plants have adapted to their environments and developed ways of luring new pollinators to their flowers. These troopers endure intense heat, biting frosts, poor soil, even salt water, and still manage to bloom.

In the lowlands of Mexico and Central America, a plant known as the bull's-horn acacia *(Acacia cornigera)* grows in partnership with a certain type of ant. The acacia has a pair of swollen thorns at the base of each leaf where a queen ant raises her young. Worker ants sip the plant's nectar, collect small nutritious growths at the tip of each leaf, and sting other insects that try to feed on the plant. Scientists believe that without its ant protectors, the acacia would die of insect damage within a few months.

On Lava Rock

Haleakela, the largest volcano on the island of Maui in Hawaii, is home to a bizarre-looking flowering plant called *Argyroxiphium sandwicense*. It is better known as the silversword, or "big-headed one," after its habit of growth. At one time, so many of these plants covered the rim of Haleakela's dead crater that the area appeared silvery gray, and the lava rock was barely visible under the thick growth.

Growing 10,000 feet (3,000 m) above sea level, the silversword faces extremes of temperature. To conserve moisture during peri-ods of blistering heat, the plant has long, thin leaves covered with silvery fuzz that reflects sunlight. The leaves also contain a gelatinlike substance that makes it easier for the plant to store water efficiently.

The silversword's leaves reflect sunlight and protect the plant from its scorching environment.

Year after year, the silversword grows steadily larger until it is almost 2 feet (60 cm) in diameter. Eventually a swordlike stem grows upward to a height of up to 8 feet (2.5 m). After about twenty years, the plant blooms for the first time, and hundreds of reddish-purple flowers with yellow centers cover its stem. Bees arrive to pollinate the flowers, and slowly the seeds ripen.

Grasslands

Millions of years ago, when much of the world's climate grew hotter and drier and forests disappeared, members of the grass family adapted and spread. These angiosperms evolved deep roots that helped them survive periods of drought and lightning storms. Except for a few self-pollinated species, most grasses depended on wind—not insects or birds—to carry their pollen.

Pollen Problems

Pollen from wind-pollinated plants causes a condition known as hay fever.

Grass flowers are extremely small, almost microscopic. They do not need brash blooms or scents to attract pollinators. They have a few basic parts—stamens, which produce pollen, and pistils, which catch pollen and form seeds. The blooms of grasses are grouped in clusters called **spikelets**. Two bracts enclose each flower. The flowers open for only an

The tiny blooms of a wheat plant open for an hour or less each day—just long enough for wind to pick up their pollen.

Legend

According to a legend of the Tohono O'odham peoples, who are native to the American Southwest, a young maiden was out walking one day when she suddenly sank into the earth. In her place rose a giant cactus commonly known as the saguaro *(Carnegiea gigantea)*. O'odham people still treat the saguaro with great respect.

hour or less each day, long enough for the slightest breeze to pick up their dry, abundant pollen.

Over the centuries, the grass family has become extremely important to humans. Plants in this versatile family produce grains such as wheat, corn, rice, and rye. Sugar comes from a grass, as do many medicines, beverages, and oil.

In Deserts

The Sonoran Desert stretches north from Mexico into parts of southeastern California and southwestern Arizona. Summer temperatures rise above 100° Fahrenheit (35° Celsius); during winter, the thermometer often hovers around 70° F (20° C). This is the only place in the wild where the saguaro cactus, a 50-foot (15-m) giant, grows.

Only a few inches of rainfall come to the Sonoran Desert each season. In order to soak up this water efficiently, the saguaro's roots grow close to the surface and store moisture in pulpy stems. A tough skin, pleated like an accordion, surrounds the stems. The skin expands when the plant is filled with water and shrinks when it is empty.

Saguaros grow slowly, so slowly that a 6-inch (15-cm) plant can be 12 years old. Most do not flower until they reach age 50. In late April, during the driest part of the year, saguaros begin blooming. Delicate white flowers appear at the top of each central trunk and on the ends of each arm. They open at night, long enough for bats and moths to pollinate them, then close the next morning. Small fruit develops and, when ripe, turns reddish and provides food for many desert inhabitants.

A long-nosed bat pollinates the saguaro's flowers at night.

A single saguaro produces as many as forty million seeds in its lifetime. Because of the desert's extreme heat, lack of rain, and hungry creatures, only a few seeds are likely to develop into mature plants. Saguaros have plenty of staying power, however. It is not unusual for a healthy plant to live for two hundred years.

Watery World

Approximately eighty families of angiosperms live in the sea or in freshwater habitats. Like their relatives on land, many are pollinated either by the wind or by insects. Some flowering plants are unique, however.

Hidden just beyond many shorelines are underwater meadows of long, ribbon-shaped green leaves. They sway back and forth with the motion of the waves and offer food, shelter, and protection for a variety of sea creatures. These leaves are called eelgrass.

Eelgrass *(Zostera marina)* is not a seaweed but a flowering plant. Its roots are anchored in mud and shifting sands several feet below the surface of the water. Frequently, at low tide, the plants are exposed. Where the water is clear enough for the sun to penetrate, however, they may be found growing at depths of more than 100 feet (30 m).

The flowers of eelgrass, like those of prairie grasses, are small and hidden behind bracts. Since insects do not pollinate them, they have no need for bright colors or showy blooms. Pollen from male flowers is released into the water in long

Harvesting Eelgrass

The Seri Indians of Mexico are experts at finding eelgrass along the Gulf of California. They wait until the plants float loose near the shore; then they pull them in and spread them on the beach to dry for several days. The Seri separate the grain from the fruit and store it until it is ground into flour for gruel or bread.

chains and spread to female flowers by the waves. Seeds form, and soon new eelgrass sprouts in the mud.

Meadows of eelgrass not only provide food for a host of fish and other wildlife, but also soften the impact of waves on coastlines and prevent erosion. As the grass dies and is carried offshore, it sinks and becomes food for populations of larger animals in deeper waters.

Eelgrass provides shelter for marine animals such as this orange starfish.

Any threat to migrating pollinators, such as these monarch butterflies, has a secondary impact on flowering plants.

Chapter Five

Disappearing

The brightest, showiest, and freakiest flowers might soon disappear because many of their pollinators are endangered. During the past fifty years, the number of bee colonies in the United States has been declining at an alarming rate and is now at a critical stage. To add to the problem, Africanized honeybees—a cross between African and European bees—have invaded several states. Besides threatening people's lives, these invaders carry a parasite that can infect and kill local bees. All of this has a devastating effect on flowering plants that depend on bees for pollination.

Many migrating birds and insects need flowers and their nectar to supply them with enough energy to complete their yearly journey. More and more of the animals' "fast-food" stopovers are being cleared or destroyed to make room for roads, housing, and other types of construction. This endangers migrating creatures as well as the flowers they pollinate.

Heavy use of pesticides also threatens pollinators. The poisons in pesticides either kill the animals or affect their ability to reproduce. This impacts flowers that depend on the animals.

What does all of this mean for humans? As we have seen, many important products come from flowering plants. About a quarter of the prescription drugs in the United States contains at least one ingredient from a plant or its flowers. Scientists have studied only a small number of plants for their healing abilities, and now they are racing to examine others before the plants are destroyed.

About three thousand species of flowering plants in the United States alone are in danger of disappearing, and close to forty thousand others around the world may soon become extinct. Members of groups such as the Center for Plant Conservation (CPC), the Convention on International Trade of Endangered Species (CITES), and the WorldWide Fund for Nature are trying to preserve threatened plants and their habitats.

This dogwood plant has seen better days.

You, too, can help by finding out more about the work of these groups. Become aware of flowering plants. If you spot an unusual one, avoid picking it, especially if it is the only one of its kind in the area. Other freaky flowers are no doubt blooming near you. If you take the time to look closely at them, you might be amazed at what you see.

Glossary

angiosperm—a plant that produces seeds enclosed in a fruit

anther—the male reproductive part of a flower

binomial—a two-part scientific name that includes the genus and species of an organism

bract—a modified leaf that looks like a petal

cone—the reproductive container of a gymnosperm

cross-pollination—the transfer of pollen from the male parts of one flower to the female parts of another flower

embryo—the young plant within a seed

filament—the thin stalk that supports the anther of a flower

fruit—the ripened ovary of a flowering plant

genus—a group of closely related species

gymnosperm—a plant that produces seeds that are "naked," or not enclosed in a fruit

nectar—a sweet liquid that plants produce

ovary—the female reproductive organ of a flower

ovule—a structure in a plant's ovary that, after it is fertilized, develops into a seed

parasite—an organism that lives on or in the body of another and takes nourishment from it

pistil—the female reproductive structure of a flower

pollinator—an agent responsible for transferring pollen from male anthers to female stigmas

self-pollination—the transfer of pollen from male to female parts of the same flower

sepal—the part of a flower that encloses its petals and reproductive bodies

spadix—a club-shaped growth bearing many tiny flowers surrounded by a large bract

species—a group of closely related organisms

spikelet—a cluster of small flowers

stamen—the male reproductive part of a flower

stigma—the top part of the pistil

style—the part of a flower that grows from the ovary and holds the stigma upright

synconia—bulbous structures filled with hundreds of flowers that become fruit

To Find Out More

Books

Burton, Jane, and Kim Taylor. *The Nature and Science of Flowers*. Milwaukee: Gareth Stevens Publications, 1998.

Hershey, David. *Plant Biology Science Projects*. New York: John Wiley & Sons, 1995.

Powledge, Fred. *Pharmacy in the Forest: How Medicines Are Found in the Natural World*. New York: Atheneum, 1998.

Silverstein, Alvin, et al. *Plants*. New York: Twenty-First Century Books, 1996.

Taylor, Barbara. *Incredible Plants*. New York: DK Publishing, 1997.

Images Online

http://arboretum.fullerton.edu/cor.asp
This site shows a corpse flower in various stages of its growth.

http://www.botany.hawaii.edu/faculty/carr/silversword.htm
This site contains images of the silversword.

http://www.batcon.org
Bat Conservation International's Web site has photographs and general information about bats worldwide.

Organizations and Online Sites

The Center for Plant Conservation (CPC)
P.O. Box 299
St. Louis, MO 63166
http://www.mobot.org/CPC/
This organization works with other groups to prevent the extinction of native plants in the United States.

The Nature Conservancy
4245 N. Fairfax Drive, Suite 100
Arlington, VA 22203-1606
http://www.tnc.org/
This nonprofit group purchases and manages habitats where endangered plants grow.

World Wildlife Fund

1250 Twenty-Fourth Street NW

Washington, DC 20037

http://www.worldwildlife.org

The World Wildlife Fund is the largest privately supported international group working to protect endangered species.

A Note on Sources

Flowers have always fascinated me. Why is each one unique, and how do insects, birds, and other creatures pollinate the many different varieties? In searching for answers to these and other questions, I turned to a book recommended by a librarian: Arthur Cronquist's *The Evolution and Classification of Flowering Plants*. Another volume, *Floral Biology: Studies on Floral Evolution in Animal-Pollinated Plants*, edited by David Lloyd and Spencer Barrett, revealed more interesting facts about plants and their matchmakers.

A visit to the University of California's Botanical Gardens, with its Rain Forest House of strange plants, hillsides of African exotics, and greenhouse of meat-eating plants, gave me new insight into the diversity of flowering plants. I became anxious to discover what other unusual flowers grow around the world.

Next, I searched through natural science magazines for the studies of botanists in foreign lands. Many researchers were attempting to identify rare flowers and their pollinators before they disappear. I also visited numerous Web sites that contain facts as well as dramatic images of both common and exotic flowers. All of these sources helped in the writing of this book.

Now when I spot fields of wildflowers or see gardens in bloom, I look for clues in the color, shape, and scent of individual blooms. Each detail tells me something about why the plant looks the way it does. It also reveals something about the exciting relationship between the flower and its pollinator.

—*D. M. Souza*

Index

Numbers in *italics* indicate illustrations.

About the Author

After teaching in both middle grades and high school for several years, D. M. Souza began freelance writing. She especially enjoys writing about science topics and, in her free time, often tracks and studies the wildlife living around her solar-powered mountain cabin in Northern California. Souza has written more than two dozen books for young people, including *Meat-Eating Plants* and *What Is a Fungus?* for Franklin Watts.